The Bird Church

poems by

Marisol Cortez

Finishing Line Press
Georgetown, Kentucky

The Bird Church

Copyright © 2025 by Marisol Cortez
ISBN 979-8-89990-019-8 First Edition
All rights reserved under International and Pan-American Copyright Conventions. No part of this book may be reproduced in any manner whatsoever without written permission from the publisher, except in the case of brief quotations embodied in critical articles and reviews.

Publisher: Leah Huete de Maines
Editor: Christen Kincaid
Cover Art: Alice "Pájara" Canestaro-Garcia
Author Photo: Greg Harman
Cover Design: Elizabeth Maines McCleavy

Order online: www.finishinglinepress.com
also available on amazon.com

Author inquiries and mail orders:
Finishing Line Press
PO Box 1626
Georgetown, Kentucky 40324
USA

Contents

1. the highways whose transient towns are also homes

edge/effects ... 1
perry, OK ... 2
cars and trucks ... 4
chicharras, a/c ... 8
a prayer tie untied ... 12

2. little dolphins of the sky

at the bird church of inks lake (on the first day of the comey hearings) ... 15
found fruit ... 16
snoutnoses ... 17
fl(u)orescence ... 18
about a grackle ... 20
another poem about common birds ... 22
conservation status: least concern ... 25
just a jay (jay kay) ... 27
the wild parrots of mission road ... 28
sliver of a dream ... 34

3. seed to the wind

amazonian ... 37
águila ... 39
cosmos ... 47
first snow ... 53
rumi speaks of night travelers ... 55
to bbz who loves garbage and its trucks ...57
loyalty oath: día de los muertos, november 2020 ...58
what is here ... 62

*to jesse and wolfi
and all tiny creatures everywhere*

1. the highways whose transient towns are also homes

EDGE/EFFECTS

have you ever noticed
that the houses most close
to the highway, the holdouts,
the ones that refused to
sell, the ones held
closest to bosom
of urban industrial,
the ones
in perpetual umbra of interstate
might be

                          in fact

                          so close

                          it's as though

                                          they're remote? an odd
                                          edge effect of living
                                              inside the scar:
                                        so near, so close
                                      it's like the highway
                             skirted em after all, just
                                   left em in the dust
                               unsupervised, just look
                at all the dense winding green
                       of their yards running over
                     with chickens or children,
                         just smell the jasmine
                  or wisteria blowing through
                     wind tunnel of IH 35
                      South as from above
               it whistles, as I've said before,
          like the waves trapped in miniature
              within the enameled pink ear
                                of the conch.

PERRY, OK

a surreal sight beneath
tornadic skies: 18-wheeler
blown onto its side, cab up

in the median of
a deserted 35 South
as intersecting strangers

slam to a stop
dash across highway
clamber up cab
pry open its door

as I dial 911, my little one
in the back playing
Nintendo nonchalant

later, unexpectedly banked
in a Perry, Oklahoma chain motel
by those same tornadic skies

the rain slants inward
through window slid open
to the day's second surprise

someone's summer garden
carefully plotted out back,
the red dirt carved

from sloping green that
shrugs off the reach
of perfunctory parking lot

and runs wild into the arms
of arboreal break
whose buffering swell

like seaweed churns green
and lush in the turgid
supercharged air

to remind me that chains
are also places
where people work and live

their everyday patterns
a writing over, superscript
ordinarily invisible

from the highway whose
transient towns
are also homes.

CARS AND TRUCKS

A tiny human
comes into this world
vulnerable
dependent
unable to see more
than twelve inches
in front of his face—
the distance from his eyes
to mama's

Slowly his vision
clears, and the forms
of the world emerge,
objects of awe
to name and
exclaim over

A tiny human appears
and because of our own
programming
we cannot stop ourselves
from giving him cars
and trucks to play with

Because of our own training
we cannot stop these fictions
of gender which begin
to cleave
the tiniest human
from a primary sense
of being primate first,
human, and
not a boy
whatever that is

Now cars and trucks
and buses rivet
and sometimes
terrorize his attention
like nothing else

as they rumble up to a garbage can
or rev in the driveway before
roaring down the street
or honk for a neighbor
to come outside like
texting
had never been
invented

Tah! says my baby
boy, *Tuh! Bap bap!*
as they rumble
and roar
and rev
and honk and
smoke

And in the paper a story:
the shells of Dungoness crabs
are dissolving because
the oceans have become
so acidic. No: let me not
obscure our agency there
with passive voice:

because we
have made the oceans
so acidic
with cars
and trucks
and stacks

So when it comes down to it
isn't putting a toy car
into the hands
of a child
like handing him
toy guns to play with?

Can it really be so different
when men
and yes, it is
almost always men
use engines to scare
cyclists in a crosswalk
or shatter shared soundscapes
with glasspacks, men
who don't have to put
babies to sleep?

When it comes down to it,
is it not an insult to the tiny
humanness of boys
to give weapons as gifts?

I wish I could claw back
all cars and trucks
from my child's eager hands
Replace them instead
with bikes
or skates,
sleds
or dogs,
horses

so that my boy can stay human

I wish I could remove
all gas-fired engines
all cars
from the clutches of humans
who think they are men
whatever that means
and their companies
and their dreams
and schemes

so all humans can stay alive

I wish I could crumple up all
engines like tinfoil,
do an easy layup, shoot them
into the sun and then
fill all highways with soil
to become giant planters
or with water, to become
the world's largest
waterpark—

even tho I don't believe
in a personal politics of purity
that says if I drive
how dare I write
this poem

even tho I cannot even write
this goddamn poem because
I am always driving
when the words arrive
on time, I'm always late
despite the luxury of speed,
of space/time compression
afforded by internal combustion and
the dissolution of crab shells
somewhere in some ocean
in a story I can't bear
to read

and I have to pull over
just to set my words free
as my baby cries
in the back seat.

CHICHARRAS, A/C

My despair is a paralysis
that I never knew was there
that I never knew was
despair:
hard to put a finger on
until you sit and
settle in

It was the memory of our ride
down Military Drive
insulated from
the air outside,
over 100,
heat index 115
says George
but inside the car
is artificially
conditioned,
thank God
thank God
for that:
my last two cars
didn't have it

It is the memory of a ride
in the twilight of cars
over the river at Espada,
then caught in the throat
of a train, seeing the coal cars
crawl by en route to Calaveras
seeing Calumet's flare
over the trees

And my eldest child
in the backseat
telling me:

                                                        Hope
                                               I'm not alive
when global warming starts.

I can't bear to tell him
that it isn't *if*
any longer,
it isn't even when

I remember him standing once
outside with a moth in his hand. It had died
when it flew into the hot wax
of a candle. Outside
on the porch
he hid from us
to cry,
cradling it
in his hand,
a tiny Icarus

My heart aches, thinking
of how he loves the world
of tiny things, his eye
on the spider
and the sparrow—
and so I follow it back
and back, the ache
within me, the pain
of our failure,
until the content
drops away
to reveal
only tightness in bands
around my throat, my eyes.
Only constriction,
only salt water, echo
of oceans

until

it is suddenly plain
and I recognize
the name of it,

that it even has a name
to be spoken, a shape
my mouth can make
to pronounce it.
There it is,
that's what it is:
despair, yes,
I see you, come in.
It floats to the surface
like a paper flower
when my mind stops scrambling
for solutions   and
in the quiet
and just for a moment
I hear the high summer whirr
of chicharras outside
over the a/c. And
I hear the summer whirr
of the a/c too.
Everything is alive—
not just chicharras
—to wake

                    up

                            into

                        everything is there
                            to hold you

                            and if

                    there were only this
                in a lifetime of trance,
                    if there was only
                    one single moment
                        of stillness,
                 of waking up into
                    what is here:

			it would be enough

		it is

	enough

that it becomes
possible
again
to imagine
continuing.
For him,
for the tiniest
ones.

A PRAYER TIE UNTIED

may i forgive myself
for the ragged edge
of all i was unable to do
today. for all i left undone.

may i now allow myself
to rest.

2. little dolphins of the sky

AT THE BIRD CHURCH OF INKS LAKE (ON THE FIRST DAY OF THE COMEY HEARINGS)

If you watch something long enough
with reverence
you will want to write it down,
to capture it somehow, before
it is gone
or you are: how

the smaller dun-colored hummers
can seem to share a feeder fine

but when arrives
that one with black head,
bib of white, dull necklace of
deep plum that startles violet
in sunlight, like amethyst
corsage pinned to collar,

the others scatter quick, chittering away
like little dolphins
of the sky.

FOUND FRUIT

found a solitary small
       orange
on the ground out walking
the block, first walk postpartum
with the baby wrapped up
against the rush of viejitas
cooing and clutching
like mourning doves,
& some viejitos too—
my people, mi gente,
mi barrio. sky mid-february
gray. where'd that orange
come from, then,
       single spot of color
       blown onto the sidewalk,
no tree in sight?
last of late-winter
westside citrus,
the backyard ornamentals
too hard for viejitas
to pick. whatever
the case, i peel
and eat it
once home,
feeling pale golden
fingers of fruit
steeping like sunshine
into my milk—and boy
is it good,
almost perfect,
       a high note of tang
wild as night wind
whistling at the top
of unseen trees.

SNOUTNOSES

                    not monarchs
                    yet (it's only september)

          but snoutnoses, plain brown
      sparrows of the butterfly
world flow in columns
      over the streets
          of the westside mostly,

or so it seems, late afternoon
      and into the evening.

          for their part, the streets
              become a wind tunnel
                of small wings
                washing
                and rushing
            over the cars &
miraculously missing
      windshields by some
            unaccounted for law
                  of aerodynamics.

              whether breaking a drought
              by hatching en masse
          or migrating in a relay
of generations—minnesota
      to méxico
           —no one can say,
                not even the news

        but we
      think they look
     like raggedy autumn
leaf fall blown
     like dust
          dancing down corridor
            of west commerce.

FL(U)ORESCENCE

I watch the bees
excitedly swarm
the bright floral tubules
of the simple aloe in
complex bloom
on its single stalk
there by the fence,
its flowers an
indescribably sassy shade
of melon or coral
that makes one reach for
the nail polish names
from three half-assed months
working retail at alamo
barber & beauty
so many moons ago—
an ever-expanding catalog of product
in ever more finely-parsed shades
I cared nothing about, until now:

Santa Monica Beach Peach.
Cajun Shrimp. A Red-Vival City

I watch the bees crawl their way up
the narrow dangling fingerling
of each blossom, then beep
as they back up feet first,
little saddle bags packed
with sticky pollen the color
of flaming nail polish
sunset

It reminds me that when
I saw the bees yesterday,
pushing open the gate
to brush past amazing spire
of succulent fl(u)orescence,
I wondered where they went
at night, and thought then

to Google it, fumbling for phone
before remembering I'd left it
inside, on purpose, for precisely
this reason
of paying attention
to what is actually here

before remembering:
they go back to their hives
at night, of course, duh,
they must—but then

where
are
their
hives?

ABOUT A GRACKLE

On Drexel, grackles
crackle
like intercom scratching
its itchy throat,
like radio
static,
like—what,
walky talky?
Like scrape
of register
transaction?

But that's not quite
it, doesn't capture it,
the analogy not quite
right, not accurate,
analogy itself
is like

standing amidst fissure
between the thing itself
and the word, straining
for closure

and so simile
then
must be
a neuro
transmitter between
synapses, poetry
the crossing
of cognitive oceans,
a translation of sense
into symbol

a photography
an orthography (or,
an ornith-
ology, perhaps?

in any case:)
a lexicon
insufficient,
asymptotic,
approaching
infinity

but never quite
getting there.

Just as all language
all symbol
is rhythm
at bottom,
I've thought recently,
I remember,
standing on Drexel
astride bicycle
straining to tell you
about a grackle:

all language is
sense, is syllable,
is sibliant
is assonant
is lullaby
is song,
fundamentally
at bottom,
is sound
without content,
pitter patter
of pattern,
somatic,
presymbol, where it comes from—
the word that wells up
from the world.

ANOTHER POEM ABOUT COMMON BIRDS

I hear it
come out of me
like a poem
without trying—
so after the phone
I write it down, about how

I'm standing in front
of the oven's
hot breath, gaze
tracking upward,
past the full-page
newsprint ad that Yoko
Ono took out
in the New York Times
in memory of John

(she is a Japanese artist
I explain to Jesse, nine now,
old enough
to know John
from the Beatles, but
not Yoko Ono,
not yet)

and it is a New Year's wish
to remind us that WAR
IS OVER! (*if* you want it,
that's the catch, sly
conditional printed
in small type below)
with love
from tío John and
tía Yoko,
a small delight
to see it there in the Times,
sandwiched between stories
about Trump and Putin
Putin and Trump,

a novelty so far removed
from the dishwater dull
San Antonio Express-News
that I cut it out and tape it
to the kitchen wall, past which
my eyes now slide:

because out the kitchen window
on the roach tree out back, whose
vinegary sap attracts autumnal curtains
of American snoutnose butterflies
each fall
is one strapping tuxedo'ed blue jay,
typically nasty, obnoxious, common but
gorgeous still—striped, crested
in blue and white and black (things
you can notice when
they're not screaming
and divebombing cats
for once). First one jay
and then two
when another,
slightly larger, lights
beside the first
to perch politely upon the lip
of an old branch
so long sawed off the roach tree
it has formed a hollow,
a cavity there
for rain,
a watering hole,
a bird bar, into which
I watch the two jays
politely taking turns
dipping down
to sip
or nibble,
first one and
then the other

until

a grackle
descends, an asshole
apparently entitled
to swoop in and scatter
jays from their roost
by right of size
and seize their drink. And he
or she or they or it or
whatever neo or xeno
pronouns birds use
for themselves, or don't
is even larger and shinier
than the two robust jays,
feathers smooth
as black glass,
big as a crow or
raven, almost,
so solid and substantial
you can almost imagine
why the strangest thought
might have occurred
to the ancestors:
to snare and eat
these ancient
airborne
raptors

(but to my vegan friends:
I don't advocate the snaring
and eating of grackles
or other birds,
however common.)

CONSERVATION STATUS: LEAST CONCERN

James Brush
an Austin writer
and a good one
at that
already has a little book of poems
entirely about grackles
and vultures

Still   Once

*I saw a grackle
fly off with a whole thing
of chips in its mouth!*
says Jesse

who when a littler kid
than he is now
told me he'd want
a grackle as pet, if only
it weren't illegal.

Why would it be illegal?
I asked, thinking it must be
because grackles
deserve their freedom.
But no: *it's because
you can train a grackle
to steal,* he said,
then got mad
when I laughed
and tried to stop myself
from laughing but
laughed all the more.

And so I must throw these lines
atop my own crackling pile
of grackle poems

Conservation Status: Least Concern

is what Wikipedia reports
Quiscalus Mexicanus
has been assigned by the International Union
for the Conservation of Nature
on a seven-point scale from
extinct to abundant,
abbreviated "LC"
inside a little green circle
meaning, eh

    Still   Once

Above our heads as we walked
back from Jesse's dad's house
to ours
we saw two great-tailed grackles
explode across the sky, scattered
by a hawk or falcon diving
for its dinner

They escaped, metallic beaks
emitting their rasping robot
screeches, and with em,
I am sure, a meteor shower
of Hot Flaming Cheeto crumbs
as well

Ordinarily imperturbable
these grackles were clearly upset
tho what a majestic marvel
of a domestic drama it was
to see it unfold up close
above our barrio sidewalk

which is not to suggest
that nearly becoming falcon food
merits an upgrade in international concern
for the conservation of grackles

It was just kinda cool
is why I'm telling you.

JUST A JAY (JAY KAY)

From outside
a falcon
screams, I think—
but no, just a jay
playing at being
byrd of prey

Two, three, fucking
four times
I'm tricked

until finally
one day

farther to the North,
I hear a familiar scream and
shrug if off: *eh,*
it's just a jay

till I turn
my face skyward
and see
I've been pwned
yet again:
ancestral wings
circle on thermals
in silent
survey.

THE WILD PARROTS OF MISSION ROAD

All last night I held you
as you woke
multiple times in a panic
gasping for air
like a drowning man's head
bursting to surface

but this morning you get up
anyway: it's my birthday
and to celebrate we'll search

for some feral birds
we heard rumor of—

(many years before,
the story goes, the owner of Moore's
Feed and Seed on S. Flores
went crazy and set his birds free

Or *went sane*,
you say
with a smirk)

—Monk Parakeets, technically
but more like parrotlets there
on the parapet of pecan
or mesquite, sounding
sometimes like monkeys
sometimes like seagulls
sometimes like dolphins
or doggie toys or
the little red shoes
Jesse wore as a baby
which announced every step
with a squeak.

Via echolocation, via telephony
we have caught wind of them,
decided to look: a friend of Cat

says she spotted them last
in a stand of trees that Cat points out
as we glide over highway
where it crosses the river
one Wednesday on our
way back from class.

So we park at the park,
we trudge down the path
the city has built
exactly for Sunday
mornings like this,
for nodding your hat
at walkers, pausing
to gape at anhingas that seem
more dinosaurial
than even most birds,
their webbed feet marsupial, their
snake necks pulsing weirdly.

We migrate south beneath
the tracks to the trees
where Cat said they'd be

but they're not. Then clamber up
riverbank hill for one last longing look
beneath the canopy there,
where the only thing moving
is chicharra noise, rich and slow
as molasses. Panting hard
at the top cuz
it's too hot already
at 10am. Told you we
should've come earlier.
Defeated, we descend
just as a train
advances on the tracks
that span the river,
holding its horn

out of respect as it crawls
carefully past

but then comes a clamor
a squawking
distinct
from the swell
of swallows circling
water, not far
from adobe nests adherent
to rail-line trellis:
not swallows not sparrows
not grackles not the slow-winged
altitude of cara cara. Something
else, flying furiously south toward
Mission Concepción
where the internet said
they nest. *Parrot-shaped!*
Jesse shouts and points.
The train's rumbling passage
has rattled them loose
from invisible roost, some
screaming, some streaming grasses
or straw in their clutch
as they fly. *It's them.*

So we head for Concepción,
our bare heads cooking but
determined
to follow them
past the old mill superceded
by boarded-up power plant
itself
superceded
by multi-million-dollar plans
for clean tech incubator,
plus new apartments, for which
the neighborhood homes
are surely future parking lots

without knowing it
just yet. Past the lot where developers
cleared the ground already
by ripping out
the little Streamline trailers
like weeds, casting them
off to who knows where—
dandelion fluff
without so much as a wish.
As they did a second time
further down Mission Road
at Mission Trails, across the street

from Concepción, where it was all
set in motion, this chain of evictions
so many centuries ago
with the cutting off of hands
and tongues of original lands
whose great great great-grand
children today
have flocked—like parrots
caught and caged in a shop
—to church for mariachi mass
to sing in the language
of the crown. We're here at last.
But you are too ill
with despair to exit the car.
We'll leave it running, a/c on
and Jesse and I can ask
the Park Service rangers
where wild parrots would nest
if we need to.

But we don't need to:

we find them ourselves
laughing in the trees
outside Concepción:
four little clownfaces

grooming each other
in an old mizquitl
(that's mesquite in Nahuatl)
and two chatterboxes up
in a scrub oak.
We breathe them in—at last
we have found them
just by following
the whisper of a story,
a pointed finger, and finally
the tiny sounds and signs
themselves
of this odd bit of wildness
returned, this wildness
that softens you, opens you,
I can see it in your face when
you finally spill from the car
to see for yourself. It's like
what Ross Gay said once
after reading his poetry
for an hour at least (mostly
poems about gardening
and gratitude): I don't know
what spirituality has to do
with anything, I just know
when I'm out in the garden
I'm a little less scared
of dying.

It's like that. Every week
I could come back
to watch for hours,
my heart never full
of the sight of them
laughing—there is no end
to the words and poems I have
for them. Every Sunday,
here on pew of mizquitl
observing what remains,

what is here, until
the centuries begin
to fall away finally
from the Missions—
until the fatal spell of summer
breaks
and the blessing of rain
washes the bloody story
of a hemisphere
back to original
stone.

SLIVER OF A DREAM

hearts beat high in the tree
bees buzz low in the tree
beets grow down in the ground,
beating like hearts

3. seed to the wind

AMAZONIAN

We sleep in shifts:
me taking the early morning gray,
lavender air heavy as bergamot,
while you steal away
to plan and write
and shave your face smooth
as youth. You come back to sleep

dressed in fresh clothes
crawling beside me to cocoon
in summer light sheets
and it's my turn to wake
and it's your turn to sleep

but not before you whisper,
I know what I'm going to do now—
and you tell me your plans.

I am naked from the night before,
from where you left me. I am
naked and supple as an otter
on the banks of a river
where you have been walking
and dreaming, and I have pulled you
into the water to be with me,
one of the good humans.

One of the humans who protects my home.

No: I am a pink dolphin, Amazonian
and like the stories warn I might,
I have fallen in love with a human—
I have seen you walking
by the river in your clean clothes
and with an understanding ancient
as our kinship, as the hint
of phalanges within fins,
with a memory ancient as my hand
within yours, I understand

your longings and aspirations
and I have kidnapped you
to be with me for all time,
perhaps to transform you
out of your human body,

to free you
from all suffering and limitation,
to slip naked through sheets of water that roll
and billow like sail,
for all our remaining
days together, wake to sleep
and sleep to wake.

I must be careful to think of everything,
I say, remembering the cruel irony
of so many human myths,
remembering the story, Greek,
I think,
of the origin of crickets,
of the man who withered
away into insect
because his immortal lover,
wanting that death never part them,
thought to request
eternal life for him

but not eternal youth.

ÁGUILA

Fierce eagle, águila
I wake up early, the morning of
your burial
seized with these words
that no one dare write

You were born in 1922
the eldest of ten
son of a barber
son of a drinker
son of a man
who beat your mother
Antonia
and forced you
to be father early,
on the streets with newspapers,
shoe shines. The softness beaten
out of you. That is the reality
of colonial city
of Westside segregation
that you lived.

Child of Lanier High, Westside
where you met my grandmother—
quiet, solemn
says Mrs. Sánchez
bringing yearbook to show me una güera
in a sea of brown faces:
Slavic Mexican
Mexican Jew
ashamed to be both
ashamed to be born
outside the circle
of matrimonial sacrament
calling herself Spanish
instead.

But that was after you dropped out
and then returned to school—

I saw the video UT did
when they filmed you talking
about your growing up times,
your war experience
for their oral history
of Mexican veteranos
from World War II

One of the times you cried

was when you recounted a friend
who came to your door
insisting you go back to school:
Rudy Cortez was his name,
no relation

You had dropped out to follow
your parents your sisters
up to Arkansas
for the cotton crop
Your father had pulled
the girls
out of school
How could you stay there
without helping too

You cried then, remembering
how your friend—
six months later when
malaria sent you all
packing home, back to San Anto
—came to your door to persuade you
(you had to be persuaded)
to return and graduate
but you did

you did
and you cried
to think of it
and so did I

The other time you cried
was when you told your story
of war. *We were so naïve*, you said,
remembering.

They draped your coffin with American flag
but you hadn't wanted to go to war

You signed up not wanting to be
drafted, sent anywhere
You thought by signing up
on your own
you could stay
at home, in San Antonio—
of course of course
said the recruiter
before shipping you off
to Colorado, New York, Germany
to sit in the tail of a plane and
shoot. When you heard that pilots
were paid more
survived more often
than tailgunners
you and your friend
sprang to sign up,
to train and then test

To this day you feel
they flunked you
not because you were not
coordinated enough
like they said
but because of who you were,
where you came from.
Race the unspoken
in between lines,
race what assigns
who steers at the front
who shoots at the back
who lives who dies

without speaking
its name, without
having to

but you survived it

and you cried

remembering the cost
of that survival, remembering
Hiroshima, how
they dropped the bomb
on the eve of being shipped out
again,
this time to Pacific theater:
We're gonna die,
you told your friend,
This time
we won't make it back
home. And you knelt down,
made a bargain with God—

Please
if you let me live
I will live my life upright

—but they bombed Hiroshima
and Nagasaki
in the nick of time.
Remembering, knowing
the enormity of
what saved you,
the outline of bodies
vaporized against a wall,
which allowed you
to finally go home to San Anto
and marry Grandma,
raise fourteen kids
on postman's wages—

fourteen kids, híjole,
what were you thinking

—remembering what it cost
to survive
you cried

and so did I,

not understanding fully
until then
on whose shoulders I stood,
the great historical vehicle
of Mexicano mobility
post-war, catching all of us up
in its indifferent trawl.
Bittersweet upswing
out of that Westside barrio.

But you hadn't wanted to go to war.
Never forget that.

So you led an upright life
so upright it could hurt
like when my sister, just twelve,
sat crying silently before you
when you cracked about her weight

Like when you wrote me lamenting
my firstborn's unwed conception—*how
dare you*

And then there was the day
I went to your house
to see you, interview you
for Westside history project
and you knew where to cut
a mixed girl
right where

it hurt
the most:
I don't know why you're doing this,
you said afterwards.
*I can remember
when you didn't even
want
to think of yourself
as Mexican.*

I stood up to you then: *Oh yeah?
When was that?* Because
there has never been a time
I've not thought of myself
as Mexican.

But after I left your house
I sat in the car and shook,
ashamed as my grandma
in who I was—in between,
neither nor, not even
in my own family:
Is that really how you saw me?
Is that really what you thought?
Did you really think I didn't
see myself as part of you,
where you came from,
even as I came to you
to honor your struggle,
your suffering
your survival
and my own?

No le hace: when I went
to visit you again,
this time in the hospital,
right after this last stroke
that would eventually kill you
but before your vocal chords

collapsed, before
the feeding tube placed
when you could no longer swallow
without choking,
before you could no longer
get out of bed
or move. Before we could touch you
only with gloves
because of the staph, your body slowly
shriveling, freezing immobile
until all that was left
was the spark and barb
of your mind, ever sharp,
wagging a silent finger in warning
when they tried to get you
to sign the will.

Someone else's will,
not your own.
You'd bargained with God
for your life
and they'd have to pry it
from your hands
cold and dead.

Pero

before all that
you were surprised to see me—
Mi'jita, I didn't think you'd come.
I didn't think so
either,
I'd been angry, at
your words to me and to
my father, my sister, to all of us
wounded by your severity
without speaking back
because you were the elder,
the eldest, you were the one

who'd had to survive, whose survival
had made us all possible.
But I came. And none of it mattered.
I held your hand and you asked me
about my illegitimate son,
and if I was still riding
my bike like I did
that one time to your house,
astonishing you, and
if I was still interviewing Westsiders.
I like your blouse, you said, with knowing:
I'd bought it a few days before,
huipil from a Mexican vendor,
like the embroidered dresses
my grandma would wear.

And will you go back to Kansas?
you wanted to know, though
I've been home going on
two years now. Just making sure.
No more Kansas,
I tell you. *San Antonio
is my home.*

COSMOS

My grandma
grew cosmos
famously, a
farmer's wife who always
had kitchen garden going where
flowers grew too
in orange and yellow hues
just as vital as carotene,
color of carrots
she fed me once raw,
pulled from the ground
still tasting like soil.

I'd never had them
that way, not being
from the Midwest,
rural corner of Minnesota
where my mom
grew up on a rented farm
outside the small towns there—
not a townie tho,
like the kids from money. Still,
my mom made salutatorian—
*Would've been valedictorian too
if Anne Mears hadn't cheated,
just kidding!* she says—and that
was how she got to go
to college where
she did meet some man
and drop out to marry
just like my grandma
said she would if she
bothered with college,
only girl in the family to go
(she went back and finished,
dear reader, don't worry)
and only one to marry in color,
move back to South Texas with
my brown Tejano dad

and never go back,
never even miss
those Minnesota
winters
Minnesota is
Mnisota in Dakota Sioux
meaning sky-tinted water:
a watery place of landlocked lakes
I've never lived but whose soil
made me still, land of Line 3
cutting through manoomin
wetlands sacred to Ojibwe,
prairied land of Plum Creek
of Little House fame,
books I read too
even here in South Texas,
half Mexican and even still
never knowing the other side,
Indian side of the story.
Land of *you bet* and *I suppose*
of cornfed Woebegone
niceness now
belied and blood spattered
by Floyd's murder
Land of 1000 massacres
not so different from here, this
land of a 1000 missions
insisting
there are no Indians left, only High-
spanics. Psssht. Just look around—
where do you think brownness
comes from
anyway?

And yet

I found
in a Ziplock of clippings my mother saved
from my grandparents' NFO days

an op-ed by my Irish grandfather,
a tenant farmer,
supporting the right
of brown farmworkers to organize
out West, far far
from the Minnesota prairies where
there were no Mexicanos or Filipinos,
where farm labor
was more apt to be
white high schoolers
hired for the summer or
your own kids, working for free

But Grandpa
sided with Chávez beneath his Virgen banner
rather than follow the poisonous
siren call of whiteness
to abandon solidarity,
rather than betray
other salt of the earth
for those same corporate
interests he fought
in the National Farmers Organization

*I just finished reading
an article in your paper,
he wrote: It states
most farm operators oppose
unionization of farm labor.*

*I have news for you.
Any average farm operator
who opposes unionization
would be foolish, to
put it mildly.
What better way
could there be to curb
the steady advance
of corporate farming?*

*I see no reason
why farm labor shouldn't
have a decent living wage
like any other labor.
Signed: A farm operator,
Jim Foley, Slayton,
Minn*

And this
decades before
he could even imagine
he might have half-
Mexican grandchildren
to make it personal
instead of a matter of simply being
a good ancestor, someone
who sincerely believed
in the rights of the poor
to a decent and dignified life

And his NFO wife, my grandma
grew cosmos in her garden,
each year saving the seeds
to plant the following spring,
parsimoniously
And when she died
each child and grandchild
received a small plastic baggie
of seed, her ashes
and estate, all the wealth
that was left

which I never planted,
always moving too fast
to tend to the earth
in a physical way
whatever my politics
or lineage

Not even this this past pandemic spring
when we put in a pollinator garden
for crashing monarch populations,
the whole planet convalescing
from COVID, coughing
from carbon

Cosmos

came up anyway, half the contents
of a bag of native seed
we spilled that spring—I even
thought they were weeds at first,
decorative hybrids, the bag maybe cut
with false filler,

not realizing C. sulfureus,
a cousin to marigold, is native
to greater México, named
cosmos in the 16th century
by Spanish colonial
priests who admired
the orderly
organization of petals
about a center
(how colonial indeed,
amiright?) and took them
back to the metropole,
only to be re-imported
to this hemisphere, México
to Madrid to Mnisota
a beloved blossom
held in common by
the butterflies and bees
and abuelitas across
disparate lands

In November
you will see them

driving by on the way
to Westside Y: the evidence
in a preponderance of orange
at San Fernando Number 2
where my other ancestors lie,
the cempasuchil that marks
that day we remember
the dead

Knowing this,
I lay these words down,
scatter my inheritance, bag of seed
to the wind—

see what comes up

FIRST SNOW
(for sabra's shadows)

a precious memory,
jesse's earliest at three:
first snow outside, the
driveway dusting of
an early kansas winter

(by march, of course, it'd be
obnoxious, anachronistic,
still swirling past spring break
then melting into mud—tho
in those months I'd also find
a child's tiny gold ring, too small
for all but my southpaw pinky
winking up from the slush
one day walking home amid
my own deep depression,
single diamond, i remain
convinced, impressed
in circle of most precious metal—
in fairer weather, someone
had dropped it for me to find
and pick up, so as
not to lose heart, only
to lose it again)

but in december little jesse
had never seen the magic of water
frozen into soft dry powder—
we'd only just moved to the prairie
from a tejas mostly snowless until
the terror of last year's storm—
and he ran to scoop it up
and squeeze it,
laughing aloud
until the cold white
burned his tiny hand red
and he dropped it,
crying

it is his first memory of being alive:
that first snow, in its dualness

both blank page
and black relief of its words

both emptiness of shadow
and the substance it limns

both pain of cold
and the light that pushes from behind to turn
collapse into color, pain into craft

both nopal flash-frozen, melting into rot
both the citrus cracked, the spring bereft
of its ephemeral perfumes—

orange blossom,
mountain laurel,
redbud

—and the gift of the new growth
at the base of the tree, irrepressible

RUMI SPEAKS OF NIGHT TRAVELERS

I birthed you into
an incredible name

but then you one-upped me,
named yourself
rebirthed
yourself
by yourself
for yourself

sprang fully formed
from your own forehead:
you had to,
just to live

Night traveler. Arabic,
I tell my father's cousin
when he asks
at the funeral
what it means,
in what language,
your name.

Ah, I know
that familiar double take,
what it means when
his eyes slide
sideways
to meet his wife's
in stealth,

the questions inscribed
upon their faces

questions of ancestry
questions of gender

But later—

weeping my way
through guided
meditation, praying
for care the size
of my fear
that I am just too small
to fix it all, that
all I can do
is help you hide
until you can escape
this state

—I come to understand

what you have named
in yourself, in me
who birthed you who
birthed yourself

when the teacher tells me:

Rumi speaks of night travelers
who turn toward the darkness
and are willing to know their own fear
He says: Sit with your friends, don't go back to sleep
Life's water flows from darkness
Search the darkness, don't run from it
Night travelers are full of light

and you are too

TO BBZ WHO LOVES GARBAGE AND ITS TRUCKS

Watch you roll around on the floor singing
garbage trucks / garbage trucks oh yeah!

Never knew there were so many names for vehicular equipment—but there are excavators backhoes mixers dozers loaders trenchers cranes y más, y so much más. After your shower you want us to wrap you up in an enormous fluffy towel and coo: *It's a baby cement mixer!*

But think about the sanitation workers and the nobility of their struggle: *I Am A Man*, read their signs. And the man who operated the truck that beeped obligingly at you as he called out: *Hey papi!* He was nice. And the guy who from up high operated the crane that ate up the brush we piled on our street: how fine and precise and delicate his scraping mechanical pincer, directed in space by joystick, the delicate fingers of one who scoops the last grains of rice off a plate. He saw us watching from the sidewalk, and I hope he felt pride in his skill—for it was masterful.

Mostly I marvel at a child's fascination with the detritus of a dying industrial society, the cans and the refuse inside and the trucks and services so many have organized to demand, and rightly so. Still, all that garbage pushed inside the yawning gorge of a gigantic tip— I've seen the videos you watch—it's chilling.

But the other day we found a memory stick shaped like a small blue bin, PR swag from our public utility. You tote it everywhere, finally, a can small enough to fit in your hand as you sing, *What's inside? Garbage?* I guess, but you laugh at my laughable lack of imagination. *No! It 'cycling!* Recycling, you mean. So I laugh alongside you, saying, hands on hips: *That garbage can tricked us!*

LOYALTY OATH: DÍA DE LOS MUERTOS, NOVEMBER 2020

I pledge allegiance to birds
and Black birders
I pledge allegiance to sea turtles
and silly gulls
I pledge allegiance to yard sales,
plate sales, voguing, ancient foraging
circuits: nuez, tuna, nopal, yuca
All the gifts of this land
we once wandered, not lost
like Cabeza de Vaca, but logically
seasonally ecologically
moving. I pledge allegiance
to dewberries growing on the banks
of the lake the Army Corps made
from dammed up river
and the red hornets
who live there too, whose protective sting
to my brow while foraging
sends me reeling,
falling
backwards with the force
of a strike

I pledge allegiance to sacred springs
I pledge allegiance to every wetland
and swamp that hid runaway slaves
and Native boarding school children.
May every effort to drain you
fail, may we fill you up again
instead, restore you, so that no
White House built beneath the lash
may comfortably occupy
your Potomac slough.

I pledge allegiance to rivers
that swallow up
ill-gotten walls and
the lies that built them
I pledge allegiance to the burning forests—

Amazonian, ancient redwood
and all alveoli everywhere:
from Floyd's breath extinguished
beneath boot and badge
on a hot Minneapolis sidewalk
to the breaths of elders artificially inflated
by ventilators down in the Rio Grande Valley:
I pledge allegiance to all lungs, all breath,
arboreal or mammalian, Aeolian
winds of the body which
resist just by inspiring
exhaling
surviving

I pledge allegiance to dogs and frogs
and bikes

I pledge allegiance to the million plus
of the pandemic dead who died over Zoom
When I started this poem
on the eve of first debate
that number was 213,000
But we cannot forget
this has happened before
in San Francisco, New York,
and here, the abandoned unnamed
dead of the earliest years of AIDS
and so
I pledge allegiance to the love and rage
of the late Larry Kramer
I pledge allegiance to trans kids
and gay TikTok, to the schizophrenic homeless
on the back stoop of Starbucks
to the red-tailed hawks that swirl over
downtown despite
the disappearances of development
and redevelopment

I pledge allegiance to the intelligence
of pigs and corvids, the crows and grackles
who never forget a face

I pledge allegiance to the wonder of thriving
coral reef
taller than the Empire State Building itself
and the discovery there of *Spirula Spirula,*
never-before-seen squid
whose shell is internal,
a ram's horn coiled
inside gelatinous body,
posterior glowing
bioluminescent green
like Halloween
glo-stick

I pledge allegiance to poetry,
public libraries, senior centers,
daycare workers, mail carriers,
city pigeons, palaterías, tamaladas,
Food Not Bombs, Bayard Rustin, the rust
that claims the excavator, the sugar in
the gas tank, the microbiome that
makes our bodies mere perturbation
in the flora and forest of bacterial
pluriverse

I pledge allegiance to los chimuelos,
the youngest and oldest among us and
to the memory that persists when the body fails
and the self-organizing joy
of the toddler, moving
nonlinearly through parking lots

I pledge allegiance to the autochthonous
to sage and copal, to the four directions
to the red road, the eight fold path,
to the dream, to Dreamtime, to

Dreamers with a capital-D and
democracy lowercased

to the silence of witness

to the struggle
to the struggle
the upraised fist
but also to the softness
and stillness of the open
hand that knows
no enmity, no homeland
no loyalty

WHAT IS HERE

Yesterday it felt as though
just the turning of the year
December to January
was enough
that it could be spring
already, almost.
But today the sky
feels like crying
a cold rain.

We steal an hour
and walk along the river
holding hands.
The city has drained it
to dredge.
We see
little fish swimming
upstream past exhaustion
We see gasoline shiny
fish swimming sideways
lackadaisically
and the occasional neon koi,
muscular as forearm.
We see turtles, big and small,
their size an advantage over fish
in weathering the unaccustomed
state of an unnatural river
gone back to its natural flow—
just a trickle.
They wedge against rocks,
noses aired,
letting water course and
break over untroubled shells.
We see turtles whose names
escape us both but
whose soft flat shells
and tipped beaks
bring it right to tongue's edge.
We see speckled suckers

resting at mud's bottom,
dead or at ease.
We see unruffled ducks
standing one-legged.
We see maintenance trucks
driving along the
exposed roadway
of river bottom.
We see glasses frames in mud
when you sidle up to the edge
and make as if to jump.
We see an unknown whiteness
flowing from the open mouth
of a hotel's drainage outflow,
painting an oily passage
down water like contrails
from jets in flight.

When we walked here the other day
just a little bit north, just a little upriver,
I told you
what my father said
about the wild terror of the riverbanks
in the 1950s. About the snakes
that would scare him
out of swimming.
About the raft left tied up
for anyone to untie
and use.

But this is not a nostalgic poem
This is not a poem of lamentation
or declension
This is a poem about seeing what is
here   This is a poem about
what it is
that remains
to be seen:

                    a crowd of stunned fish
                      deposited by current
                    at the mouth of the locks
                      where the wily city
                    has figured out how to lift
                     whole boatfuls of tourists
                     so that they rise and fall
                along Hugman's constructed channel
                     like magic, as though
                         the river's flow
                            ran even
                         and unbroken.

ACKNOWLEDGMENTS

My gratitude to the many magazines, journals and venues which previously published the following poems from this collection:

An earlier version of "Águila" appeared in the December 2014/January 2015 issue of *La Voz de Esperanza*.

"About a Grackle" appeared as "Meditation on Creation 3: About a Grackle" in the Winter 2017 issue of *Metafore Magazine*.

"Chicharras/AC" appeared in the August 2017 issue of *Voices de la Luna: A Quarterly Poetry and Arts Magazine*.

"Conservation Status: Least Concern," "Another Poem about Common Birds," "At the Bird Church," and "The Wild Parrots of Mission Road" appeared in *Words for Birds 2020: Poetics for Pandemics,* published by Deceleration at https://deceleration.news/words-for-birds-2020-pandemics/.

"Found Fruit" appeared in *The Book of Asra and Wolfi: Adventures in Reproduction*, a DIY-pubbed chapbook.

"First Snow" appeared as part of Sabra Booth's February 2021 ArtPace exhibit *Snow Shadows*.

"Loyalty Oath: Día de los Muertos, November 2020" appeared in *Gathering: A Women Who Submit Anthology,* November 2021.

Video performances of "Cars and Trucks," "Found Fruit," "First Snow," and "Cosmos" appeared in *URBAN-15*'s 2021 and 2022 productions of Mega Corazón.

"Rumi Speaks of Night Travelers" quotes from Tara Brach's dharma talk "Fear as a Pathway to Loving Presence."

Rooted in San Antonio, **Marisol Cortez** writes across genre about place and power for all the other borderwalking weirdos out there. In 2020 she published her debut novel *Luz at Midnight* (FlowerSong Press), which won the Texas Institute of Letter's 2021 Sergio Troncoso Award for First Book of Fiction and the Association for the Study of Literature and Environment's 2022 Creative Book Award. She is also the author of *I Call on the Earth* (Double Drop Press 2019), a chapbook of documentary poetry that bears witness to the forced removal of Mission Trails Mobile Home Community. Other poems and prose have appeared in *Mom Egg Review, Mutha Magazine, About Place Journal, Orion, Vice Canada, Caigibi, Metaphor Magazine, Outsider Poetry, Voices de la Luna, and La Voz de Esperanza,* among other anthologies and journals. She is co-editor of *Deceleration*, an online journal of environmental justice thought and praxis, and a fierce mama of two who writes to resist all forms of domination and remember the land. For updates on projects and publications, visit mcortez.net.

www.ingramcontent.com/pod-product-compliance
Lightning Source LLC
Chambersburg PA
CBHW030057170426
43197CB00010B/1567